HUBERT LEW

MAKE MONEY FROM ONLINE COURSE

The Comprehensive Guide on How to Launch Your Own Online Course and Turn Your Expertise into Profits

Descrierea CIP a Bibliotecii Naţionale a României
HUBERT LEW
    MAKE MONEY FROM ONLINE COURSE. The
Comprehensive Guide on How to Launch Your Own Online
Course and Turn Your Expertise into Profits / Hubert Lew –
Bucharest: Editura My Ebook, 2021
    ISBN

HUBERT LEW

MAKE MONEY FROM ONLINE COURSE

The Comprehensive Guide on How to Launch Your Own Online Course and Turn Your Expertise into Profits

My Ebook Publishing House
Bucharest, 2021

TABLE OF CONTENTS

INTRODUCTION

Have you been thinking about launching your own online course but don't know where to begin? If so, you're not alone.

Many people are curious about online course launching but put it off out of fear and anxiety. Little do they know that they are missing out on a lot of money and freedom by allowing their fears to stop them from creating their online course.

Why should you create an online course? Well, according to statistics from Coursera (an online learning platform), online learning has grown significantly in March – April, 2020.

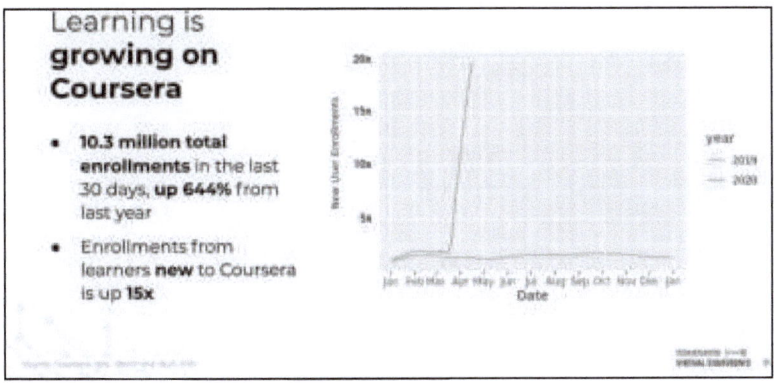

Though creating an online course requires some tech know-how, the benefits of building an online course greatly outweigh the negatives. The reason for this is that online course creators are making a full-time living selling their online courses. This incredible monetary payoff is worth the effort of creating an online course. All the while, education is increased for the students!

Luckily for you, launching an online course does not have to be difficult. With the help of this guide, you will learn key aspects of a successful online course launch. Let's get started!

Chapter 1

The Basics of an Online Course

Before launching your online course, it is important to know the basics of online courses. Knowing these basics will allow you to determine if an online course is right for you and what you should be striving for in terms of online course creation. In this chapter, we will look at what an online course entails, the benefits of creating an online course, and the attributes of a successful online course.

What is an Online Course?

An online course is a mini tutoring session or class that you can take from the comfort of your home. These courses can be on a number of different topics, ranging from yoga to calculus.

These courses are created and taught by a number of professionals, which includes PhDs and hobbyists. To put it simply, online courses are often created by academics and hobbyists alike and accessed via a mobile device, tablet, or web browser.

What makes online courses so great is that they can be enjoyed from your home at your own pace. What this means is that you do not have to have a lot of time to take an online course. All you need is a way to access the course and internet connection. You can take it at your own pace, and you do not have to be embarrassed if you are starting from scratch on the topic.

Another great benefit of online courses is that they can be free or cost little. This allows more people to gain a deeper understanding of a topic without spending a lot of money on classes. Additionally, some of these courses even offer certifications, which can be used to boost resumes or experiences.

How online courses work is that a creator uses their knowledge or experience in a particular topic to create lesson plans that are uploaded online. These lesson plans can include worksheets, readings, or video tutorials. They put these resources on a platform or website that potential customers can reach and then use.

Benefits of an Online Course

Online courses are beneficial for a number of reasons. They are beneficial to both the student and the creator. Here is why:

Online courses are beneficial to the students because it allows them easy access to more information. These courses can be used alone to further a student's knowledge, or they can be used in junction with another class to help the student better understand the topic as a whole. More so, many online courses are free, which allows students to get an education without going into more debt.

At the same time, online courses are very beneficial to the creator as well. The reason for this is that many creators make money on their courses. On average, online course creators make between $1,000 and $5,000 a month on their online courses, but some creators make more than that. In fact, online learning is expected to reach more than $240 billion by 2021.

Attributes of a Successful Online Course

In order for the creator to make money off their online course, the course must have several attributes. Without these attributes, customers will immediately assume that the online course may not be worth their time or money. Here are the attributes of a successful online course:

- **Quality Content**: Online courses must have quality content. In other words, the content must be factually accurate and up-to-date. If the content is not relevant, students will not waste their money on it.

- **Multimedia Use**: Another attribute of a successful online course is the use of multiple media outlets. Since it is online, you have access to a number of different learning tools. And since there are many different types of learners, you should use a variety of multimedia tools in order to reach the most amount of students possible.

- **Good Pacing**: Successful online courses also have correct pacing. What this means is that the course needs to be structured so that way it is neither overwhelming nor underwhelming. You want to make the lesson sizes digestible but challenging at the same time.

- **User-Friendly Setup**: A user-friendly setup is another attribute of successful online courses. You do not want your students confused about where to go or what to do. Instead, they should be able to figure it out themselves because of the user-friendly setup.

• **Self-Directed**: The final attribute of a successful online course is that it is self-directed. What this means is that the student has to have enough space to be able to go at their own pace and learn the way that they see fit. The reason for this is that most online students are busy and need to be able to tailor the course to their busy lives.

Is an Online Course Right for You?

With this in mind, you may be wondering, "Is an online course right for me?" To help you better answer this question, here is a series of questions you should ask yourself:

• Am I passionate about a particular topic?

• Am I highly knowledgeable or skilled on a particular topic?

• Do I want to help other people learn about a skill?

• Would I still teach people on this topic even if I wasn't getting paid?

If you answered yes to all four questions, then creating an online course is right for you. Even if you are unfamiliar with online course creation or technological skills, do not worry. The rest of this guide is designed to help you learn key tricks to creating a financially successful online course.

Chapter 2

Creating the Perfect Topic, Learning Outcomes, and Course Goals

To begin creating a successful online course, you must come up with the perfect topic, engaging learning outcomes, and quantifiable course goals for yourself. Without these three things, your online course will lack direction, which makes it less successful and engaging for both you and your students.

Picking the Perfect Topic

The first step to creating an online course is picking the perfect topic. This topic should be one that you are passionate about, knowledgeable on, and in high demand on the market. If the topic fails to meet any one of these three criteria, then it is not the perfect topic. Here is how to decide on the best topic for your online course:

First and foremost, you must be passionate about the topic you are teaching on. If you are not passionate about it, that will be reflected in your online course. As a result, your course will be bland and boring. If you are not interested in the topic, how can you expect your students to be?

Furthermore, if you plan on doing this type of business long-term and you're not passionate about the topic, it will lead to burnout and unhappiness.

You can ask yourself the following questions to help to figure out where your passions lie:

- What do I love doing?
- What do I love sharing with other people?
- What do other people go to me for?
- What do I look forward to doing in my life?
- What do I wish other people cared more about?

With these questions, you should create a list of potential course topics based on passion alone.

Additionally, you must be knowledgeable about the topic as well. You can be knowledgeable on a topic either from your educational background, work experience, or hobbies. Just make sure that you are knowledgeable enough that you can create accurate, up-to-date content and answer any questions that may arise. Here are some questions to figure out your expertise:

- What is my degree in?
- What skills have I developed through work?
- What skills do I already teach others about?

After answering these questions, create a list of topics that you are educated enough to teach on. If there are any topics that fall both under your passions and education lists, then you should move on to the third phase of topic selection: researching the market demand.

The topic must be in high demand in the market. You do not want to select a topic that only you care about. If you do this, your course will be unsuccessful because not many students will be interested in learning about the topic. Here is how you can test the demand for a topic:

- See if there are courses on the same topic
- Research future demands of the topic
- Presell your course idea

This exercise is simply to brainstorm to get some ideas for your potential online course topic so don't feel like you need to get it right at the start.

After you research the demand for your topics, select the topic that you are passionate about, educated on, and has the highest market demand.

Create Engaging Learning Outcomes

The next step to creating a successful online course is creating engaging learning outcomes. Learning outcomes are direct yet engaging sentences that tell potential customers exactly what they will learn from your course. If you do not have good learning outcomes, fewer people will purchase your product. Here's why:

Have you ever looked at a product and were unsure about what the product actually offers you? Chances are, you did not buy that product. The same goes for online courses. If customers do not understand the offerings of your course, they will not buy it.

In order for customers to purchase your course, they must believe that the course offers them something unique that they can use in their lives. More specifically, customers must have a clear idea of what they will get from your course and why they should take yours over another online course.

The best way to convince a customer to take your course is to create engaging and informative learning outcomes.

When drafting your learning outcomes, think about the most important things that the student will take away from the course. You do not want to add filler topics in your learning outcomes. Instead, make sure that the learning outcomes are tailored to the course's main topic and parallel the course's title.

As you write course outcomes, you want the sentences to be punchy, informative, and engaging. Make sure to use action verbs and be confident in the phrasing. Do not use filler words. Additionally, be detailed in what the course offers. Think about answering "What, how, and why?" when creating the course outcomes.

Let's take a look at some course outcome examples:

Imagine that your online course is about "Time Management." Here is an example of a bad learning outcome: "Learn how to manage your time." This learning outcome is bad because it does not tell the reader how they will learn to manage their time. Instead, this learning outcome simply restates the topic of the course.

Here is a better version of the same learning outcome: "Learn how to manage your time by using tested time management techniques such as color-coded agendas." This learning outcome is better because it tells the reader exactly what they will learn in the course.

How To Create a Clear and Quantifiable Goal For Your Online Course

In addition to the learning outcomes, you also need to set course goals for yourself. Course goals are goals that you set for yourself and your online course. They are incredibly important because they will give you a quantifiable direction and allow you to evaluate the success of your online course. In other words, course goals are meant to give you direction and give you something to chase after.

When creating course goals, you want them to be **clear** and **quantifiable**. If they are not quantifiable, you will have no way of consistently gauging the success of your online course. Include numbers and hard facts into these course goals.

Let us look at examples of good and bad course goals:

Here is an example of a bad course goal: "Make money from the online course." This is a bad course goal because it is not specific. Though you may make some money and check this goal off your list, it does not give you a clear direction. You want your course goals to give you clear direction so you can accurately gauge the effectiveness of the course.

Here is a better version of that same course goal: "Make $1,000 from this online course," or "Sell course to 40 customers at $25 each." This goal is much better because it is easily measured and will allow you to easily quantify the success of your online course.

Chapter 3

Engaging Your Target Audience and Preselling

Another important factor in creating a successful online course is being able to engage with your target audience and presell your course. Without doing these things, you may waste a lot of time on a course that eventually does not sell. Engaging your audience and preselling ensures that enough people are interested so that you meet your course goals.

Target Audience

One of the first things to decide when creating an online is the target audience. If you do not have a clear idea of who the course is for, your course could feel disorganized, and you might have trouble marketing it to potential customers. So, it is imperative to know your intended audience from the beginning of online course creation.

Remember this quote:

If you're creating a course for everyone, then you're creating it for no one.

For example, if your course is about improving soccer skills, you will probably be catering to a younger audience. In contrast, you'll probably be catering to an older audience if you are writing about saving for retirement. It is very important to know who you were selling to before you sell your product.

Creating a Customer Avatar

A helpful assignment to do is to create a customer avatar. In other words, you want to create a profile of your ideal customer. Get clear on the demographics, geographics, and psychographics of your target audience.

For example:

What is their occupation? Where are they located? What is their age?

What is their gender? What's their average salary?

What is their education level? What is their marital status?

What books do they read? What blogs do they go to? Who do they look up to?

What are their goals and aspirations?

What are their current problems and challenges?

What courses have they bought or tried before?

What were the pros and cons?

The best way to do this exercise is to picture that one person who is your ideal customer.

If you want to take it a step further, approach a potential customer and see if he/she would like to spare half an hour to help you create your customer avatar.

How To Engage Potential Customers and Build Buzz Around Your Online Course

Once you know your intended audience, you should start engaging them through social media and other channels such as email marketing. This step not only helps to build your presence and credibility online, it also builds buzz around your soon-to-be online course.

You can engage your audience by posting about it on multiple social media accounts and sending out emails based on followers. You want to spend time on social media platforms where your audience is spending most of their time. Consider the following platforms:

- Instagram

- Facebook and Facebook Groups

- LinkedIn groups

- Quora

- Reddit

- Twitter

Additionally, you can also join particular forums around your topics. Search for "[TOPIC] + forums" on Google to find a list of related forums around your topic. For example, *"digital marketing forums"*.

When using these different platforms, it is important to immerse your product in a number of different settings. Try linking up with potential customers in chat groups related to the course topic or share your course in an actual classroom setting. No matter what, just try to expose your course to as many relevant audience members as possible.

When you engage your audience, you want to inform them about the learning outcomes and topic of your online course. The goal is to get as many people interested as possible. So, let them know about the learning outcomes immediately. Be clear about what they will get from this course and why they should want your course specifically.

In fact, it is a great idea to list learning outcomes in all social media posts. This will allow customers to immediately recognize your product and increase the chances of them remembering the course.

You can also engage potential customers via email marketing. In fact, email marketing is one of the most effective ways of communicating with potential customers and convincing them to purchase your product. We will get more into email marketing later.

Preselling Your Online Course

Once you begin engaging potential customers, you should take that opportunity to presell your online course. In short, preselling means that you pitch the course to potential customers before the actual course is made. You will pitch the course by using the learning outcomes.

Though selling a product before it is made may sound wonky, it is actually very common. Crowdfunding is a very popular example of a market that is based on preselling products. So, don't let fear or anxiety stop you from preselling your course.

In fact, all course creators should focus on preselling their products because of its numerous benefits. Most notably, preselling will allow you to gauge interest in a topic. Based on the interest during the preselling phase, you can decide to continue with the course or to change the topic. If you find that nobody is interested in this topic, you will be able to save yourself a lot of time and energy. So, you should presell in order to gauge interest and see if a topic is worth your time.

Before preselling your product, set a course goal about the minimum number of presold courses. In other words, decide on the number of courses you have to presell in order to continue with the topic. Having a concrete number before you start will prevent you from having to create a pros and cons list of whether to continue with a course topic.

If your minimum number is met or surpassed, then you should continue creating your course as planned. If your minimum goal is not met, then you should scrap the course idea. In this case, you should simply refund any customers who purchased the course, explain to them that too few people were interested, and start working on a different online course idea.

To try to generate more interest in your product, you can offer discounts or additional features to the course to those who purchase during the preselling phase. Doing this will result in more customers. Another great idea is offering a discount for those who share your product on their social media accounts. This will not only give them a discount but also allow your product to reach more people.

Chapter 4

Building Revenue from the Beginning

From the beginning phases of your online course creation, you should be planning how you plan to generate revenue from the course. If you do not know your payment expectations from the beginning, you may go over- budget on tools or simply not set the course up for optimal revenue. So, you should start planning your revenue from the beginning phases of your online course.

Create a High Converting Sales Page

The best way to make money from your online course is to have a high converting sales page. Your sales page will tell your students if you put in an adequate amount of time and money to create a high functioning course. If the sales page is faulty, the student will assume that the course is faulty as well and not purchase your product.

As a result, you must put emphasis on creating a high converting sales page. If you don't, do not expect to gain many students. Once this high converting sales page is set up, you can start selling and marketing your course during any phase of the online course launch.

In fact, you should create a high functioning sales page before you presell. If you do not have a sales page during presell, potential customers may think they are being scammed and not buy your product.

Deciding on and Sticking to a Model

Before selling your course, you also need to decide on a payment model and stick to it. In fact, you should try to keep your payment model consistent through all your courses because it makes a consistent, user- friendly experience. It is very important to decide and follow through with your model. If not, students will be confused by the payment options and they may not come back for a second course. The most popular payment options include upfront charging, certifications, and additional features.

Charge Upfront

The most popular payment option is charging upfront for the course. This means that the student must pay for the course before they have any access to its contents. Most people are familiar with this payment option, especially in the education field. Think about college. Students have to pay a tuition fee before attending classes. Charging upfront for your course works the same way.

This strategy is often very successful because it eliminates the problem of students forgetting to pay later on and is intuitive. Additionally, if you implement this on all your courses, there's a higher chance that you will gain repeat customers.

Certifications

Another great payment option is providing the course for free but only allowing a certification if the student pays. This strategy is very helpful because it allows students to test out the course before purchasing, which gives you more opportunities to prove to them why they need this course.

Additionally, this payment option is very effective because it boosts your professional credibility. Offering a certification shows that you mean business and know what you're talking about. As a result, more people will be interested in your product, which will result in more customers.

Additional Features

You can even tap on more financial options by providing optional features. These optional features can include one on one tutoring sessions, personalized homework review, or additional resources. These additional features will provide the students with a more holistic learning experience.

The main thing to keep in mind if you choose to add optional features is that you need to be able to live up to these features. Do not promise features that you will not be able to perform. For example, you should not offer individualized tutoring sessions if you know you are busy and might not be able to schedule time for these sessions.

Preselling

The first way to make and see the money from your online course is to presell the product. As we've already discussed, preselling your online course includes selling it before you create any of the content. You sell the product based on the learning outcomes and topic.

Preselling your online course is a great idea because it allows you to generate revenue before you even start on the project. If you have enough participants, you will be able to use the money that you made from preselling the course to purchase more advanced tools and create a better quality course. Or, you may already have all the tools you need. If this is the case for you, you can simply pocket the money that you've made from the presale.

Chapter 5

Choose The Right Online Course Platform

The next step to creating a financially successful online course is finding the right platform. Online course strategies have developed a lot over the years, which means there's a lot of options for you to choose from. All options come with their own benefits and negatives. So, it is important to find the best platform for your financial budget and course needs. Here are the most popular options today:

Best Course Platforms and Learning Management Systems (LMS)

One important decision that you must make about your online course is how to upload it onto the internet. You will upload it via a platform. In general, you have two main platform options: self-hosted or hosted. Let's go through each of them below.

Self-Hosted Online Course Site

One way that you can host your online course is through your own website. The benefit of hosting your course on your own website is that you have complete ownership over the site, do not have to pay a lot of money for its use, and can better brand your products.

Many new creators find creating their website difficult because they do not have any experience in coding or web development. This difficulty often causes new creators to immediately turn to an all-in-one platform (which we will discuss next). But this is not necessary. You can create your own website with no coding experience.

The most popular way to create your own website is through **WordPress**. WordPress is an open-sourced Content Management System (CMS), which is a software application that is used to manage, create, and modify digital content. WordPress is the most popular because it is free to use, easy to learn, and powerful when used correctly. In fact, 30% of the internet uses WordPress, and that includes big companies like the Walt Disney Company and Home Depot.

You should use plugins designed for online learning to optimize your website. If you publish your website online and realize you need to make some tweaks, don't worry. WordPress is easy to correct and modify down the line.

Here are some recommended online course plug-ins for Wordpress:

WP Courseware

https://flyplugins.com/wp-courseware/

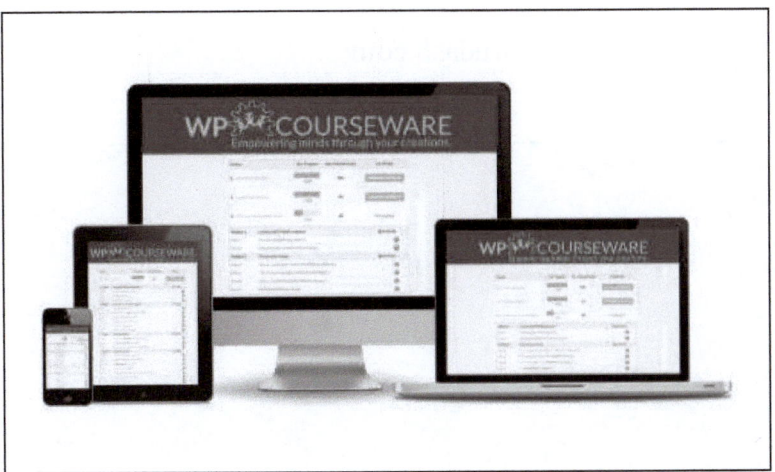

MemberMouse

https://membermouse.com/

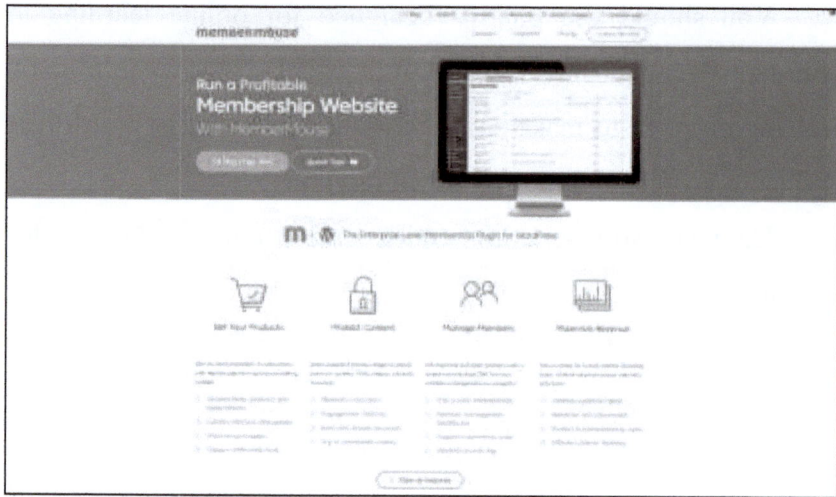

LearnDash

https://www.learndash.com/

LearnPress

https://wordpress.org/plugins/learnpress/

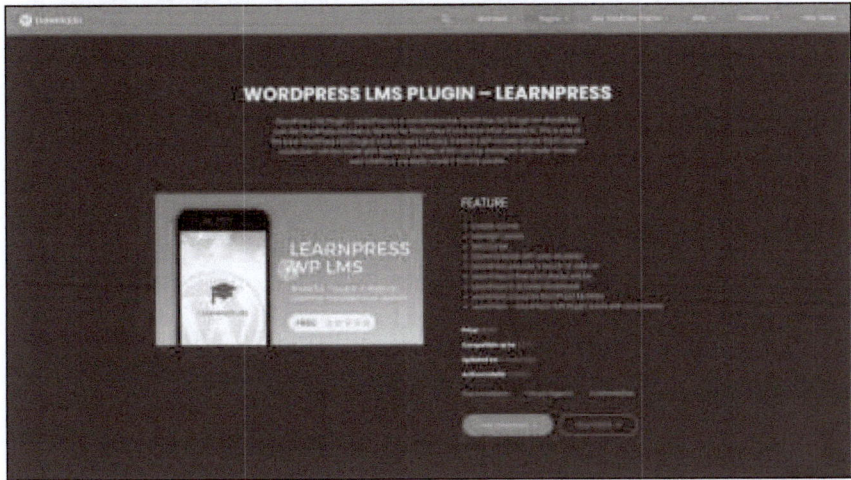

LifterLMS

https://lifterlms.com/

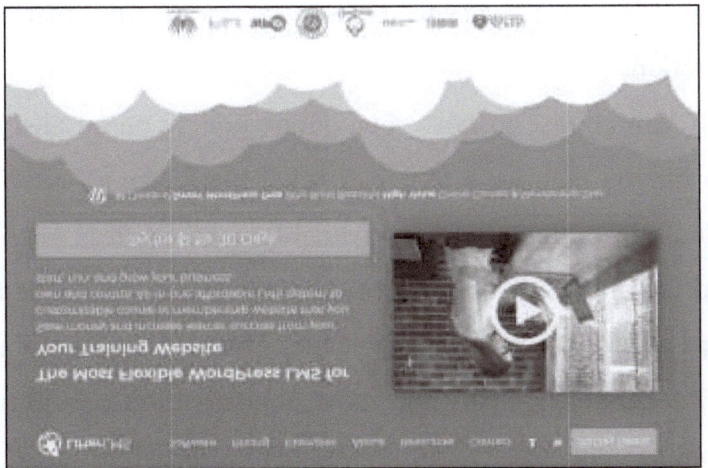

Hosted All-In-One Online Course Platform

If you are new to online courses, you may prefer an all-in-one platform hosted by a third-party. These platforms are designed for LMS solutions because they provide everything you may need for your online course. This includes formats, fonts, sales page, and more. The downside of all-in-one platforms is that you have to pay a monthly a yearly subscription to use their service, do not have full control over your site, or are limited in how you interact with customers.

Many creators are willing to sacrifice the money, ownership, and freedom for the flexibility and accessibility that all-in-one platforms provide. Unlike creating your own website, using an all-in-one platform will allow you to better focus on the content since the website design is up to the platform's jurisdiction.

If you choose to host your online course on an all-in-one platform, you then have to decide what platfoßrm to use. There are plenty of online platforms available now. So, it is important to find the one that's best for your course and budget. The three most popular platforms are Teachable, Thinkific, and Kajabi.

Teachable is easily the most popular all-in-one platform for online courses. It is extremely affordable, creates a professional look, and is user-friendly. Additionally, many students prefer the look and access of Teachable over other all-in-one platform options.

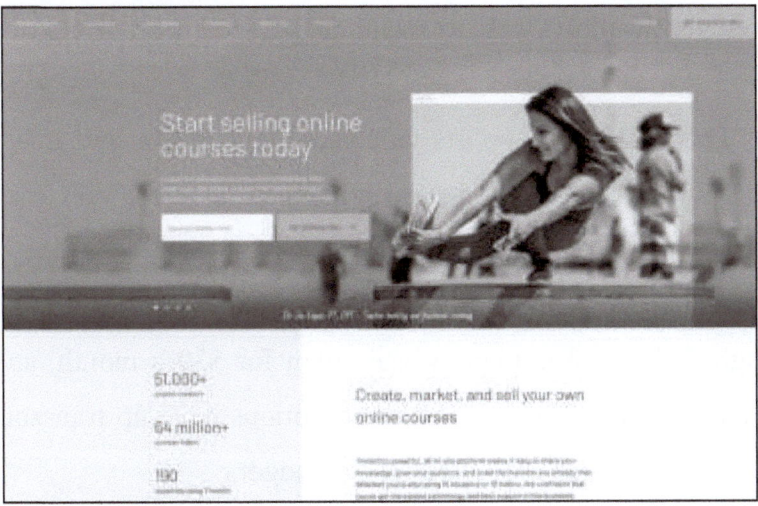

This platform supports videos, audios, PDFs, and images. Teachable also comes with a sales page builder, offers affiliate additions, and can handle the payment and taxes if you set it up as such. In other words, it allows you to customize your course without the hassle of creating your own website.

Teachable is also more affordable than other all-in-one platforms. You have the choice to select from four different payment plans. If you make $1,000 or more on your courses a month, it is recommended to use the professional plan over the free or basic plan.

Thinkific is also a popular all-in-one platform. In many aspects, it is comparable to Teachable, but it has fewer users. Thinkific can help you to create, market, and sell online courses. Better yet, it allows you to maintain your own brand and own your customer base.

This platform supports videos, audios, PDFs, and images. It also allows you to build a sales page and content very easily. So, this platform is very similar to Teachable.

Thinkific stands out from Teachable in its affordability though. It has a free plan, a basic plan for $39 a month, and a pro plan for $79 a month. All three options have no transaction fees, which is great for creators on a budget.

Kajabi is another great all-in-one online course platform. With Kajabi, you can create and market your online course, create and market your own website, host webinars, and use it as an email marketing advisor. So, it is truly an all-in-one platform.

Like the other two platforms, Kajabi supports videos, audios, PDFs, and images, all of which are forms you should use in your online course. The downside of Kajabi is that it is much more expensive than the other two options. The basic plan is around $119 a month. With that, you can only add 3 products and have 1 admin user.

Chapter 6

Planning Course Content

Once you have created your plan, presold your course, and found the right platform, it is time to move on to course content creation. The course content is what your students will see, use, and learn from when participating in the course. It is important that your content is factually accurate, engaging, and visually attractive in order to keep students interested and come back for more courses.

When you are planning your course content, you must think about multimedia content types, outlining, and content creation tools.

Multimedia Content Types

The first step of creating your course content is deciding what type of multimedia you want to use. In short, multimedia use is when you use a variety of media tools in your course. This includes PDFs, audios, videos, PowerPoints, and more. For online courses, it is important to use a number of media types to keep students captivated and engaged by the content.

Videos

Videos are the most popular form of media for online courses. The reason that they are popular is that they give the students something to look at while they are learning. Since they are learning from their computers, they can get distracted easily. The videos keep their eyes trained on the lesson though, which helps to prevent distractions.

There are several ways you can use videos in your lessons. If you want to demonstrate a skill or talk as though you were giving a lecture, then you can just show your body or face. This will give your students a face-to-face like interaction through the screen.

If you need to show numbers or have a PowerPoint, you can also use a screen recording with a Voice Over. This option will allow you to show the students your computer screen while you explain what they are looking at. This option is great for math courses or something that involves a lot of quotes.

A third way you can use videos is through animation. If you want to have an entertaining tutorial-style course, animating your videos is a great way to provide snippets of video information.

Worksheets

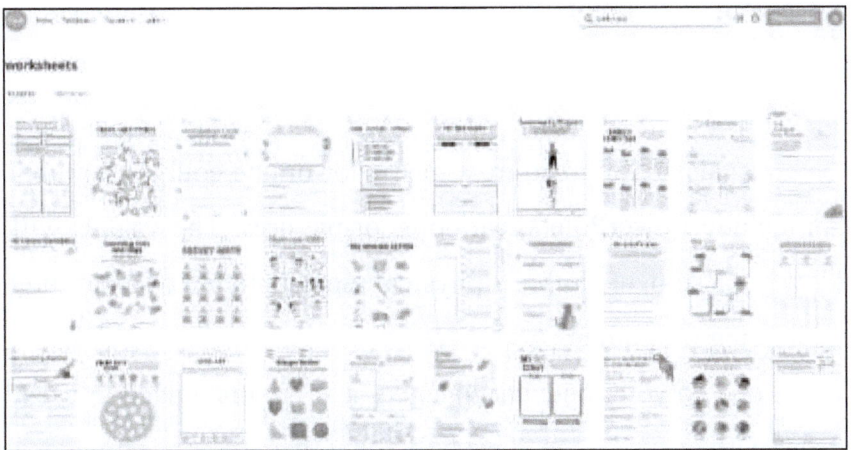

Worksheets are another highly popular medium for online courses. You can use worksheets to distribute information, create cheat sheets, or homework. The point of worksheets is to give your students a tangible study tool that they can download and print for later.

When you upload worksheets, you want to offer more than one download type. It is recommended to upload a Word and a

PDF copy of all worksheets. This ensures that all students have access to download the content.

Even though videos are the most popular tools for online students, you absolutely must upload worksheets for your students. The reason for this is that most learners need to write out the information and challenge themselves in order to learn the information long term.

Visuals

Visuals are another great media for online courses. Visuals can include PowerPoints, cartoons, or pictures. The visuals will allow your students to see a physical representation of what they are hearing or reading.

To keep your students engaged, it is recommended to use a visual with every lesson. This will allow them to connect an idea with an image, which will improve the likeliness that they remember the content.

Audio

Another media outlet you can use is audio. This media is less popular than the other two simply because most learners do not retain information auditorily. None the less, audios can be extremely helpful in the right contexts.

If your course is designed for on-the-go use, then you should consider using audios. The audios will allow your students to listen to the course almost like they would a podcast. They could listen to your course in the car, waiting in line, or at the gym.

Planning Your Content

Once you know what multimedia you want to use, you should start planning your course. Planning your content includes researching and outlining for the course. This step is crucial to creating a course that this professional, accurate, and reputable.

As you plan your content, make sure that all your lesson plans match up with the learning outcomes. If your plans do not match, either change the learning outcomes or change the plans. It is important that the two match in order to ensure that students get what they pay for and come back for more of your courses later on.

Research

The first step to planning your content is researching. It is assumed that you already know some things about your topic, but you still want to research it to make sure you are correct and up-to-date on the content. Read and watch content that is created by experts.

In the research phase, it is also helpful to watch other online courses on similar topics. What do those creators say? What do they think is important? This will help you to gauge where your focus should be in your course lessons.

Additionally, let the research go its own course. Instead of trying to find specific answers or opinions on the topic, read as much as possible, and research thoroughly. This will ensure that you are getting the most accurate picture of the topic, and it will allow you to answer questions better later on.

Outline

Once you have completed the research phase, you should move on to outlining. The point of the outline is to start grouping topics and ideas together for the lesson plans. At this point, the sections and groupings do not need to be exact. Instead, the outline is to help you get your thoughts together.

In the outline, you want to separate topics so that you can start creating lesson units. These lesson units will fill the weeks that your online course is live. It is important that the contents of each unit are relevant to the main unit but still connect to the course as a whole.

When you are outlining, think of a natural progression of the information. Is there any information that the students must know first before moving on? Often vocabulary or a general overview of the topic goes first.

Best Content Creation Tools

In addition to choosing a platform, you also need to select correct content creation tools. These types of tools include PDF makers, cameras, microphones, and more. In other words, these tools will allow you to create beautiful content that you can then upload on your website or platform.

Here is what you should look out for:

Video Recording Tools

Some of the most important content creation tools are video recording tools. These tools will allow you to record yourself instructing on or demonstrating a skill to your online students. If you create an online course, you certainly should record yourself. The reason for this is that over half of online students prefer to watch a video than read a document. Here are popular video recording tools:

APowerSoft Free Online Screen Recorder is a software tool that will allow you to screen record. This is beneficial if you need to do a Voice Over while showing a PowerPoint. This tool is free and easy to use.

ScreenFlow I another screen recording tool but specifically for Mac users.

Camtasia is the most popular screen recording tool for both PC and Mac users.

Smart Phones are another great video recording tool. They say the best camera you have is the one you already have, which in most cases is your smart phone. They are extremely convenient if you already have one and are very straight forward to use. In addition, you will be able to incorporate other editing tools with your phone for even more convenience.

A webcam such as Logitech's range of webcams are a great choice if you are going to record from your computer.

Zoom. If your online course's format going to be "conference style", Zoom is the best tool for that.

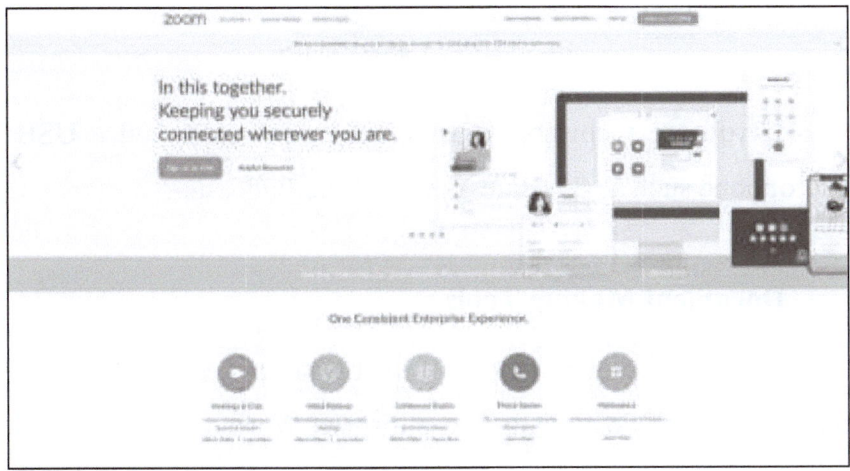

In addition to these tools, consider purchasing a **microphone** and **lighting** for an optimal visual and audio experience.

If you are recording your screen, we recommend a USB microphone such as the Blue Yeti or Rode Podcaster.

Document Making Tools

In addition to uploading videos or audios, you will almost certainly upload documents in the form of Word or PDF.

Here are some recommended tools to create your documents:

- Microsoft Word

- OpenOffice

- Google Docs

- **Canva** is the most popular design tool. It allows you to create a number of documents like ebooks, checklists, presentations, and more. It has a lot of options to choose from, is user-friendly, and comes in free and premium payment options.

Editing Tools

Finally, once you have created your content, you will want to edit it before publication. Luckily, there are a lot of editing options on the market today. Here are the two most popular:

Grammarly is one of the best tools for editing written content. You can either use the free option or upgrade to a payment plan if you need more assistance. You can either use Grammarly on the web or download it on your phone, tablet, or laptop.

iMovie is a great video editing tool for Mac users which comes pre- installed. It is more user-friendly than other video software, making it great for beginners.

Adobe Premier Pro. If you're a bit more savvy, Premier Pro is the way to go. There are a lot of video tutorials on YouTube to help you learn the basics of Adobe.

Chapter 7

Creating Lesson Plans and Course Content

One of the most important steps to creating your online course is having a killer lesson plan. The point of a lesson plan is to give you a definitive script to go off of when you create the content. If your lesson plans are unclear or lack all the information needed, your course content will seem disoriented and unprofessional. So, it is very important to create the best lesson plans.

You create your lesson plans based on the multimedia content, outline, and creation tools that we discussed in the last chapter. You will want the lesson plan to explicitly state the multimedia type, the exact phrasing, and include the learning objectives for each individual lesson. Here is how to create a killer lesson plan:

1. Decide on the Media for Each Lesson

The first step to creating your lesson plan is to decide on the media for each lesson. This must be the first step of every lesson plan because the media type will affect how you present the information. As a result, you will either speak or write differently depending on the media. You simply select media type based on your preferences and the content you are teaching.

Will it be in a keynote format or will you be talking in front of the camera?

2. Create a General Outline for Every Lesson

Once you know the media type you plan to use, you should create a general outline for each lesson. Creating a general outline will allow you to better place content so that way it maximizes the student's potential for comprehending the material.

Here is the order of most general outlines:

- **Introduction**: Introduce the topic, explain who this lesson is meant for, and say why this topic is important. It is important that you use the introduction to allow students to get a general understanding of exactly what is going to happen in this lesson.

- **Key Point Overview**: Explicitly state what the student is supposed to learn from the topic. "The goal of this lesson is…"

- **Lesson Overview**: Provide students with an overview of the lesson. "In this lesson, we will cover…" List every main topic of the lesson.

- **Section 1**: Section 1 is your first main point. Add a visual or worksheet.

- **Section 2**: Section 2 is your second main point. Add a visual or worksheet.

- **Section 3**: Section 3 is your third main point. Add a visual or worksheet.

- **Conclusion**: Restate the point of the lesson and give a general overview of the main topics discussed. End by providing an alternative view, asking a question, or giving a glimpse of what you will cover in your next lesson.

Of course, your outline does not have to be exactly like the one provided. In contrast, your outline should be tailored to your needs and course.

3. Script out Every Lesson Word for Word (Optional but recommended)

Once you have the general outline for your course, script out what you want to teach in each individual lesson. This means that you should write down exactly what you plan to do, say, or print. Do not leave open spaces for you to improvise. Be as specific as possible.

If you are using a video or audio file, plan out exactly what you want to say, including your greeting, examples, and sign-off. This will prevent you from using filler words or sounding awkward as you speak.

For documents, type out exactly what the document entails. This will allow you to edit the document over multiple rounds, which will ensure that the content is accurate and contains no typos.

4. Record or Make Content

After your script is planned out, it is time to actually make the content. This includes typing files, creating PowerPoints, or recording yourself.

Chapter 8

How to Launch

Once your course content is all made, it is time to start launching your product. Launching your online course includes marketing your product, having a soft launch, and doing final cleanups. Depending on how you've been marketing during your set up, launching your online course can take a few days to several weeks to complete. Let's look at the key steps to finally launching your online course.

Marketing Tactics

The first thing to do is to amp up your marketing techniques. You should continue doing what you did to engage customers during the preselling phase. At the same time, you should amp up those marketing tactics in order to reach more people than before.

Email Marketing

The most successful marketing tactic is email marketing. Of course, there are other avenues and we will get to that later. You should create an extensive email list that you've gathered from the preselling phase, continued marketing, and other avenues.

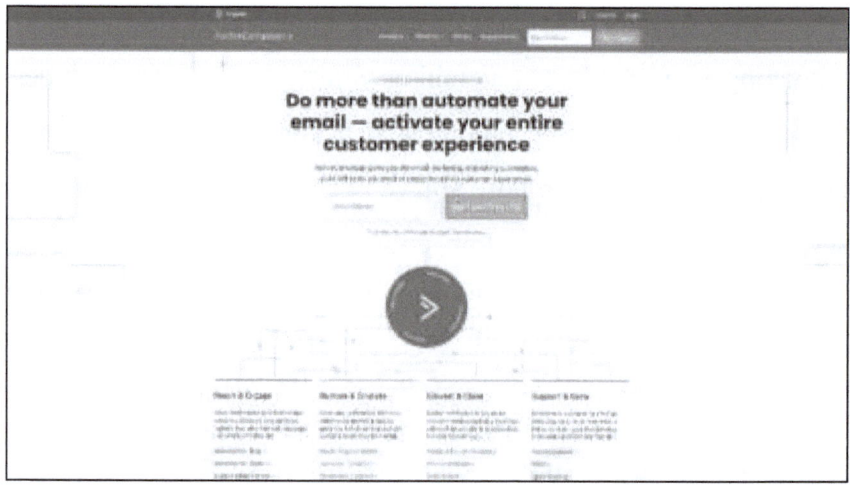

Firstly, you will need an email marketing platform such as ActiveCampaign, AWeber, or ConvertKit in order to build and send out emails to your subscribers. So make sure you sign up to one of those or an alternative.

To create an email marketing strategy, begin by creating an email account for your course. Do not use your personal email such as johndoe@gmail.com. Additionally, create a lead magnet for your email that you send out to your email list. A lead magnet is something that the customers get for signing up for your emails. A free cheat sheet or workbook is a great lead magnet.

Once you have crafted the perfect email that includes a lead magnet, you're free to send out your email to your email list.

Social Media Marketing

Since your course will be online, another great way to market your course is through multiple promotional platforms. Use as many social media sites and blogs as possible in order to reach a wide variety of audiences. Keep your branding consistent and use a professional yet educated and engaging voice. Write with active verbs.

You can use tools like Canva to create banners and different flyers to post on social media sites. Using visual aids in your social media posts is a great idea because it will catch more peoples' eyes, which in turn will result in more customers.

Influencer Marketing

What's also worthwhile is to connect with others in your industry. This is also called influencer marketing where you reach out to social media influencers to partner with you. You could offer incentives such as a commission via an affiliate program, free access to your product, and offering discount coupons for their followers. This will help you get more customers since social media influencers tend to have more followers than the average person or course creator.

Get started by following relevant influencers on platforms such as Instagram, YouTube, and LinkedIn. You can use its search feature to search for specific hashtags relevant to your niche. For example, if your niche is around leadership, then do a search for "leadership" on the platform. From there, you can follow the accounts of those in the niche.

You want to prepare an influencer outreach proposal stating the perks and benefits of promoting your online course. Here is a template you can use as a guide:

https://grin.co/blog/instagram-influencer-outreach-templates/

Paid Advertising

If you have an ad budget, consider promoting your online course through Facebook Ads and Instagram Ads. Also consider

YouTube Ads and Google Ads. The best part about most of these advertising channels is that you only pay per click and that you can set a daily ad budget. You are also given the option to narrow your target audience based on geographical location, demographics, and psychographics. This is a huge factor since you only want your ad to be shown to people who have a higher chance of buying your course.

Soft Launch

Before the launch of your online course, it is recommended to have a soft launch. A soft launch is when you allow a select group of people to start the course early in order to make sure that everything runs smoothly and there are no technical issues. A soft launch is a great way to get more customers and ensure that your product is high caliber.

In order to gain customers through a soft launch, you should offer a discount for participating in the soft launch. Explain to the customers that this is a trial run to make sure that your course runs correctly. In exchange for their cooperation, they get a discount on the course. This is a great way to get more customers while also improving your product.

You may also want to see if other course creators are interested in your soft launch. Having other course creators participate will allow you to get feedback from someone else who is experienced in creating courses. They may have key tips or insights that a student would not think to tell.

During the soft launch, make notes of any complaints or issues that customers see with the product. Once the soft launch is over, you will be able to fix everything before your final launch. Do not get your feelings hurt if students come back with complaints that you do not agree with. Simply thank them for their help and make changes accordingly.

Final Clean Up

After gathering information about your product during the soft launch, it is time to clean up all remaining issues before your final launch. This includes grammatical errors, content errors, or technical issues. Make sure to be diligent when cleaning up your course, or else customers might think that the finished product is unpolished and unprofessional.

Once you think that all of your content is correct, go back and check one more time. Chances are, there are one or two more errors. Listen to the documents, read the documents, listen to your videos, and test out any features or quizzes.

After you have gone through and checked all your content one last time, you can go ahead and launch your course. Even after the course launches though, it is important to continue marketing. If you stop marketing, you will stop getting students. Even though the launch already happened, you still want to attract more customers so that they may be interested in more courses you do down the line.

CONCLUSION

As we have seen, there are a lot of reasons that you should create an online course. Even if you are inexperienced with online content or feel that you are not educated enough to be a course creator, you still have a great chance of making a financially successful online course.

In this guide, we provide you with every step you need to take in order to launch a profitable online course.

To begin, you need to know the basics of courses and know why you want to make one. From there, you should create the perfect topic, learning outcomes, and course goals in order to attract potential customers and give yourself a clear idea of what you want from the course.

After that, you should start engaging intended audiences and preselling your product. This ensures that your product is desirable, and you don't waste time on a course that doesn't sell. Once you know that your course is marketable, you can start planning your financial goals and building revenue from the beginning.

From there, it is time to start building your online course. You should find the right platform to host your course and plan the course content. Finally, create your lesson plans and course content, continue marketing, and have a soft launch for your product. After that, you should be able to fix any minor issues and then launch your online course.

Once you have done all that, you should start seeing money from your online course! Be patient at the beginning, continue marketing, and learn from your mistakes.

Printed by Libri Plureos GmbH in Hamburg, Germany